D1267645

THE BOOK OF JAMES

Rose Visual Bible Studies

ROSE
PUBLISHING

The Book of James
Rose Visual Bible Studies

©2018 Rose Publishing, LLC

Published by Rose Publishing
An imprint of Tyndale House Ministries
Carol Stream, Illinois
www.hendricksonrose.com

ISBN 978-1-62862-758-9

All rights reserved. No part of this work may be reproduced or transmitted in any form or by any means, electronic or mechanical, including photocopying, recording, or by any information storage and retrieval system, without permission in writing from the publisher.

Scriptures taken from the Holy Bible, New International Version®, NIV®. Copyright © 1973, 1978, 1984, 2011 by Biblica, Inc.™ Used by permission of Zondervan. All rights reserved worldwide. www.zondervan.com The "NIV" and "New International Version" are trademarks registered in the United States Patent and Trademark Office by Biblica, Inc.™

Scripture quotations marked NLT are taken from the Holy Bible, New Living Translation, copyright ©1996, 2004, 2007, 2013, 2015 by Tyndale House Foundation. Used by permission of Tyndale House Publishers, Inc., Carol Stream, Illinois 60188. All rights reserved.

Author: Len Woods

Book design by Cristalle Kishi.

Images used under license from Shutterstock.com and Lightstock, LLC.

Printed in the United States of America
020323VP

Contents

"You know that the testing of your faith produces perseverance."

James 1:3

The Book of James

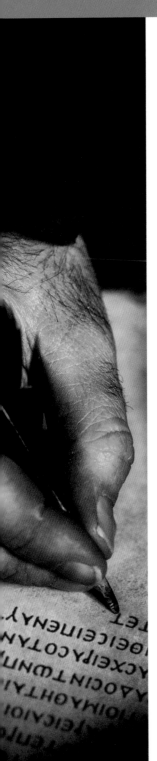

It's controversial. It features a blunt, in-your-face style. It mentions the name of *Jesus* just two times.

For these reasons and others, critics have challenged whether the book of James should even be in the Bible! It was one of the last books of the New Testament to be officially recognized as divinely inspired Scripture—and still it was questioned centuries later by some theologians.

Perhaps the book faced so much skepticism, in part, because its author, James, was unafraid to take on contentious topics in the church—things like prejudice, faith vs. works, and the reality of suffering.

All the critics aside, thank God, we have this pointed, pithy, practical letter. Many people note how it is reminiscent of the Old Testament book of Proverbs. Like Proverbs, the epistle of James speaks about everyday issues of faith in very down-to-earth terms. The imagery is graphic, but not flowery. The tone is serious. And the book's insights? *Priceless.*

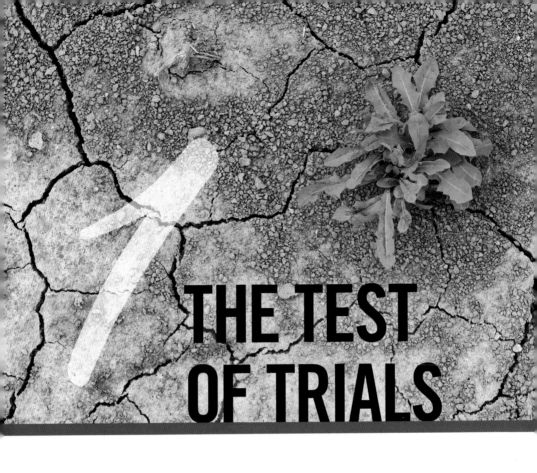

THE TEST
OF TRIALS

*Whoever Said Following
Christ Was Easy?*

JAMES 1:1–27

The Test of Trials

We all know what a test is. It's something that reveals the quality or nature or true condition of something else. For example, a history test can show how well a student understands the causes and effects of World War II. Or a stress test can reveal how healthy one's heart is.

In the book of James, the author seems to be talking about tests of a different sort—tests of faith. James addresses a variety of common tests of faith that believers face.

In this study, we'll look at six realities from life—six tests, if you will—that, according to James, reveal how healthy and mature our faith is. These are the tests of:

1. Trials
2. Favoritism
3. Good works
4. Speech
5. Relationships
6. Prayer

In this first session, we'll look at the test of trials. What's their purpose? What do trials reveal about our character? How should we think about and respond to hard times?

Read It

Key Bible Passage

For this session, read James 1:1–27.

Optional Reading

Read the entire book of James in one sitting. Why do that? Here's three reasons to read the epistle of James all at once.

1. This is surely the way the first-century Christians read it. Consider this: when you get a letter, do you read a sentence or paragraph one day, then put the letter away and say, "I'll read a few more sentences tomorrow"? No, you read the entire thing at once.

2. It's short—only about 2,300 words, equal to about half a chapter in the average non-fiction book. Bottom line? The exercise will only take you 10–15 minutes.

3. Doing so will give you an overview of the flow of the book. Seeing the big picture, the 30,000-foot view of James, will help in the same way that looking at the box top of a jigsaw puzzle is useful in beginning to see how all those individual pieces fit together.

After you read, consider:

- What are your first, overall impressions of James?

- What words jump out at you?

- What themes do you notice?

- What is the style or tone of the book?

Know It

1. According to James, are trials a matter of *if* or a matter of *when*? What's the right response to trials? What is their effect?

2. If we are not sure how to interpret our trials—our tough situations—or how to respond to them, what does James tell believers to do?

3. After discussing how to endure trials and resist temptations, James switches gears at verse 19 and focuses on the kind of life that pleases God. What are some of the positive behaviors and habits James mentions in 1:19–27? How might these be helpful when facing hard times?

Explore It

Who Was James?

The New Testament mentions several individuals named James.

- James, the brother of John and the son of Zebedee, who was among Jesus' first handpicked disciples (Mark 1:19–20)

- James, the son of Alphaeus, one of the original twelve disciples (Mark 3:18)

- James, the father of Judas (not Judas Iscariot, see Luke 6:16)

- James the younger (or James the less) (Mark 15:40)

- James, the half-brother of Jesus (Mark 6:3)

For a variety of reasons, many scholars are convinced the author of the book of James was none other than the half-brother of Jesus. James' epistle (letter) was one of the earliest written epistles in the New Testament—likely composed around AD 49. Church tradition says James was martyred in Jerusalem in AD 62.

In the early fourth century AD, the church historian Eusebius—relying on the memories of Hegesippus, who lived shortly after the apostles—referred to James as "James the Just" and by the nickname "camel knees" because James is said to have prayed so much that he developed calluses on his knees. Here is what the Bible says about him:

- During Jesus' ministry, James was not a follower of his half-brother (John 7:5).

- He personally saw the resurrected Christ (1 Corinthians 15:7).

- After Jesus' ascension into heaven, James was among the believers who gathered for a focused time of prayer (Acts 1:14).

- When the apostle Peter left Jerusalem, James became viewed as the leader there (Acts 12:17).

- The apostle Paul called James a "pillar" of the church (Galatians 2:9).

- We last see James in the New Testament meeting with Paul in Acts 21:18.

His Letter

The book of James isn't so much a book as it is a letter (or epistle). James wrote his letter to believers (most of whom were Jews) scattered across the Roman Empire (James 1:1). There are twenty-one epistles in the New Testament. The apostle Paul authored thirteen of those epistles, and the remaining, known as *general epistles,* were written by other apostles and early church leaders. James' epistle—one of the general epistles—was likely intended to be circulated among many churches, and so it addresses many practical matters facing Christians everywhere.

What It Means to Persevere

Perseverance. Endurance. Resilience. Grit. Staying power. It's this quality, as much as any other, that helps form great character. The Greek word in James 1:3, translated as *perseverance* or *endurance,* is *hypomonen.* It's from the verb *hypomeno,* which is a combination of *hypo,* meaning "under," and the verb *meno,* meaning "to remain or stay."

A good illustration of perseverance is the athlete who *remains under* the tutelage of a strength and conditioning coach, *remains under* a strict diet and workout regimen, and *remains under* barbells loaded with heavy weights day after day. All this "remaining under" (even when he or she feels like quitting) combines over time to create a powerful and tough individual who is ready for any challenge that comes when the game begins.

James is saying that trials in life function like a strenuous spiritual workout. If we throw in the proverbial towel and throw up our hands, we will never grow or get stronger. On the other hand, if we remain under the hard circumstances that our good and sovereign God has either orchestrated or allowed to come our way—and if we resolve to "work out" our faith "with fear and trembling" (Philippians 2:12)—we will increase in maturity and strength.

"Listen to Your Brother!"

If you grew up with an older sibling who was a "model child," perhaps your parents asked you, "Why can't you be more like your sister?" Or maybe they said, "You should listen more to your older brother!" If so, you know how frustrating this feels. If you're like most people, this kind of scolding only served to make you *less* inclined to give your sibling the time of day.

Was this sibling dynamic present in James' household? No one knows. However, we do know that his older half-brother Jesus was without sin (Hebrews 4:15) and that he wowed the teachers of the law at the temple in Jerusalem with his spiritual insights at age twelve (Luke 2:46–50). Later, when Jesus began his ministry of preaching, teaching, and healing, James and his siblings apparently didn't think too highly of their eldest brother. In fact, they concluded he was "out of his mind" (Mark 3:21). It wasn't until after the resurrection that everything clicked for James and his faith was born (1 Corinthians 15:7; Acts 1:14).

Following his conversion, it's interesting to see how many of Jesus' themes James repeats in his own epistle. He never explicitly quotes Jesus, but notice the impact of Jesus' words on James. It seems he did listen to his older brother after all.

JESUS	JAMES
"Blessed are the poor in spirit" (Matthew 5:3).	"Has not God chosen those who are poor?" (James 2:5).
"Blessed are those who mourn" (Matthew 5:4).	"Grieve, mourn and wail. Change your laughter into mourning" (James 4:9).
"Blessed are the merciful" (Matthew 5:7).	"Judgment without mercy will be shown to anyone who has not been merciful" (James 2:13).
"Blessed are the peacemakers" (Matthew 5:9).	"Peacemakers who sow in peace reap a harvest of righteousness" (James 3:18).
"When people insult you, persecute you . . . rejoice and be glad" (Matthew 5:11–12).	"Consider it pure joy . . . whenever you face trials of many kinds" (James 1:2).
"Anyone who is angry . . . will be subject to judgment" (Matthew 5:22).	"Human anger does not produce the righteousness that God desires" (James 1:20).
"By their fruit you will recognize them" (Matthew 7:16).	"Can a fig tree bear olives, or a grapevine bear figs?" (James 3:12).

JESUS	JAMES
"Be perfect, therefore, as your heavenly Father is perfect" (Matthew 5:48).	"Let perseverance finish its work so that you may be mature and complete, not lacking anything" (James 1:4).
"Do not store up for yourselves treasure on earth where moths and vermin destroy" (Matthew 6:19).	"Your wealth has rotted and moths have eaten your clothes" (James 5:2).
"No one can serve two masters" (Matthew 6:24).	"Friendship with the world means enmity against God" (James 4:4).
"Do not worry about tomorrow" (Matthew 6:34).	"You do not even know what will happen tomorrow" (James 4:13–14).
"Do not judge" (Matthew 7:1).	"There is only one Lawgiver and Judge. . . . Who are you to judge your neighbor?" (James 4:12).
"Your Father in heaven gives good gifts to those who ask him!" (Matthew 7:11).	"Every good and perfect gift is from above" (James 1:17).

Live It

Doing the Word

James 1:22 says, "Do not merely listen to the word, and so deceive yourselves. Do what it says." When it comes to God's Word, there are many actions we can take. We can, as James mentions, listen to it preached. We can also read Scripture for ourselves, study it, memorize it, meditate on it. We can gather in groups to discuss it. We can even distribute the Bible and try to teach its message to others. All of these are good activities.

But the most important action? Doing what the Word says! Living it out. Obeying it. Aligning our lives to its teaching. This is sometimes known as *application*, the ongoing process of surrendering to the truth and authority of God's Word.

In application, we ask questions like, "What is this passage calling me to do? Is there some new truth I need to embrace? A promise I need to stand upon as I face my current trials? A sin I need to forsake? A warning I need to heed? A reminder I need to tuck away? A quality I need to cultivate? A good example I need to follow? A bad example I need to avoid?

"Anyone who listens to the word but does not do what it says is like someone who looks at his face in a mirror and, after looking at himself, goes away and immediately forgets what he looks like."

JAMES 1:23–24

The bottom line is this: God didn't give us his Word so that we could accumulate a lot of spiritual information. He gave it so that we can undergo spiritual transformation. By all means, read the Bible. But more than that, let the Bible read you. Let its teachings shape and animate your life.

It's not enough to have a faith that *thinks* correctly . . .

<u>or</u> a faith that *feels* deeply.

We must also have a faith that *acts* obediently.

Life Application Questions

1. What are some common trials in life? What are some ways people try to run away from them rather than "remain under" them?

2. Who is someone you admire for his or her ability to persevere? How does this person respond to trials?

3. What are some ways that certain trials in your past have strengthened your faith or caused you to grow spiritually?

4. What trials and temptations are you facing in your life right now? How are you responding to them?

5. How might God be using your present trials to bring about a good outcome?

6. What are your regular habits with regard to God's Word (reading, studying, memorizing, etc.)? What specific scriptural truths are you currently attempting to put into action?

Trial or Temptation?

Bible scholars often point out that the Greek word for *trial* (James 1:2, 12) and for *temptation* (1:13–14) is the same: *peirasmos*.

- The word *trial* carries the idea of "a test that proves the quality of something."

- The word *temptation* conveys the nuance of "solicitation to evil."

James makes it clear that while God does test our faith with trials, he *never* tempts us to do evil. Trials only turn into temptations when they come upon ungodly desires lurking within us.

For example, suppose you're going through a financial crisis. God might want to use it to test and grow your faith in his provision. The enemy will try to use that trial to tempt you to succumb to bitterness, envy, or lying about your financial circumstances.

Spend some time praying for divine strength against these enticements to evil.

A Prayer When Facing Trials

Dear Lord,

I am facing _____.

I am feeling _____ about this trial.

I need _____ from you.

Help me to resist the temptation to _____.

Help me to trust in you during this trial—no matter what.

In this, as in all things, not my will, but yours be done.

Amen.

Notes

THE TEST OF FAVORITISM

Loving Our Favorite Neighbors Only?

JAMES 2:1–13

The Test of Favoritism

Before you start reading this week's passage in James, let's start with a hypothetical. What do you think would be the reaction of the people in your church if the following individuals showed up for services this coming Sunday?

- A wealthy businessman with a reputation for giving to non-profits

- A dirty, smelly homeless person

- A large group that is racially different from most in your congregation

- A group of ex-convicts from a nearby halfway house

- A married gay couple with two adopted children

- A progressive politician running for Congress

- A conservative politician running for Congress

- A well-known Christian author

- A young woman covered in body piercings and body art (tattoos)

- The chief of police and his family

- A large family with special-needs kids

What are the marks of a solid, growing faith? In chapter one, James argued that maturing believers persevere in and through the test of trials. They look to God for the wisdom needed to endure, and they make it their goal to be people of God's Word. They seek not just to know God's Word, but to do it.

In this session, we'll look at the test of favoritism. How people respond to those who are different from themselves is a clear indicator of how mature they are in their faith.

Key Bible Passage

For this session, read James 2:1–13.

Optional Reading

Read Luke 10:25–37 where Jesus answers the question "Who is my neighbor?" with an unforgettable story.

"Suppose a man comes into your meeting wearing a gold ring and fine clothes, and a poor man in filthy old clothes also comes in."

JAMES 2:2

Know It

1. In James' hypothetical scenario of a well-dressed man and a shabbily-dressed man, what might be some reasons the Christians want to give the best seat in the house to the man who appears wealthy?

2. According to James, how does God view those who are "poor in the eyes of the world" (verse 5)? (Hint: Go back and reread James 1:27.)

3. What is the royal law in verse 8, and what does living by it give (see verse 12)? How so?

James and the Law

Several times in James' letter, he mentions the *law*.

- The "perfect law that gives freedom" (or "law of liberty") (1:25; 2:12)

- The "royal law" (2:8)

What do these phrases mean? To answer correctly, we have to remember that when Jesus was asked which of the 613 positive and negative commandments of the Jewish law was paramount, he gave a two-part answer: Love God supremely, and love one's neighbors selflessly (Matthew 22:37–40).

Later, while with his disciples the night before the crucifixion, Jesus said, "A new command I give you: Love one another. As I have loved you, so you must love one another" (John 13:34). It's this *law of love* that is to be the guiding principle for those who follow Jesus. This is the *royal law*, the law of King Jesus. And it's a *perfect law* that gives freedom. We are not bound by hundreds of rules. We are liberated by the One who is Love in order to love others (1 John 4:16).

This is why James denounced prejudice and favoritism in the church. It violates Jesus' royal law of love.

The "Different" Test

Most people tend by some secret law of human nature to gravitate toward those who are *like* them. If we don't fight this tendency, over time we become more and more leery of associating with those who are *unlike* us. Experience shows that this kind of wariness and mistrust can lead to discrimination and prejudice— and that can take many forms.

In Christian community however, the Lord's call is to celebrate all we have in common and to see beyond our differences. Echoing James' denunciation of favoritism in the church, the apostle Paul writes, "There is neither Jew nor Gentile, neither slave nor free, nor is there male and female, for you are all one in Christ Jesus" (Galatians 3:28).

Work through this chart and see which kinds of differences you have the easiest and hardest time with in your relationships and interactions. (1 being the most easy and 5 the most difficult.)

ENGAGING WITH SOMEONE . . .	← Really easy for me		Really hard for me →		
Of a different race or ethnicity	1	2	3	4	5
Who has a different educational background	1	2	3	4	5
Who is at a different financial status	1	2	3	4	5
Who holds different religious beliefs	1	2	3	4	5

ENGAGING WITH SOMEONE . . .	← Really easy for me		Really hard for me →		
Who looks different (hair, fashion, body art, etc.)	1	2	3	4	5
Who is in a different political party	1	2	3	4	5
Who is from a different culture	1	2	3	4	5
Who expresses different views on divisive social issues	1	2	3	4	5
Who is differently abled than yourself (physically or mentally)	1	2	3	4	5
Who lives by a vastly different set of morals and values	1	2	3	4	5
Who has different ideas about health, diet, and fitness	1	2	3	4	5
Who is in a different age group	1	2	3	4	5
Who has different tastes in books, music, hobbies, etc.	1	2	3	4	5

The Ugly Language and Practice of Prejudice

Prejudice is the act of prejudging a person or group, deciding and forming opinions beforehand, apart from experience or knowledge. Favoritism is the giving of preferential treatment to one person or group, to the detriment of others. Here are some related words that speak of similarly ugly human behaviors.

PRESUPPOSITIONS	Assumptions made beforehand, apart from facts or real-life experience
STEREOTYPING	Viewing a person or group in a broad, sweeping, overly simplistic way
LABELING	Categorizing people, often simplistically and inaccurately, usually in order to more easily dismiss and/or restrict (sometimes known as pigeonholing)
BIAS	Unfair favor or disfavor shown to a person or group
BIGOTRY	Intolerance toward those who hold different opinions than oneself
DISCRIMINATION	Mistreating or excluding a person or group, usually on the basis of race, gender, age, religious affiliation, or political philosophy
SEGREGATION	The practice of dividing people or groups on the basis of some actual or perceived difference

Live It

The Way of the World

It is the way of the world to judge (even prejudge), label, rank, and then either include or exclude certain people or groups. Cliques and the so-called "in" group are real things. It is the way of the world for those *in* or *with* power to discriminate subtly (or not so subtly) against those who are "down the food chain" or who "don't measure up"—and at the same time, to take care of their friends. It is the way of the world to show preferential treatment to some

and harbor dismissive or even bad attitudes toward others.

How should a follower of Jesus think about and act in the following situations in light of James' warning against the sin of favoritism?

- You're grilling with a group of neighbors and they begin talking disparagingly about the new family up the block who are from another country.

- You've had three people apply for the open position in your small business. Two are evenly qualified—an attractive, young single mom and a burly ex-convict. The third is slightly less qualified. However, he is the son of a friend, and she keeps calling to tell you how much he could really use the work.

- As you lament the speeding ticket you got over the weekend, your friend smiles and says, "I know the sheriff in that county. In fact, he was one of my best friends in high school. Let me make a phone call."

- Somebody gave you two tickets to the big concert. Your long-time friend would love to go. He's a huge fan. But you also could invite your boss—after all, your annual job review is coming up.

Look at the Heart

In the Old Testament book of 1 Samuel, we read about the prophet Samuel's mission to anoint a king for the nation of Israel (16:1–13).

Spotting the tall, good-looking Eliab, Samuel concluded, "Surely, he must be the one." But God said to Samuel, "Do not consider his appearance or his height, for I have rejected him. The LORD does not look at the things people look at. People look at the outward appearance, *but the LORD looks at the heart*" (1 Samuel 16:7, emphasis added).

Life Application Questions

1. Even those who aren't believers in Jesus are struck by how accepting he was of those who were often shunned and discriminated against in first-century Jewish culture: Samaritans, Gentiles, women, children, prostitutes, tax collectors, lepers, etc. What's a story from the New Testament in which Jesus showed kindness to someone considered an outcast? Why did you choose that particular story?

2. James 2:1–13 focuses on one area of favoritism: the area of wealth. What are some other areas where playing favorites happens?

3. Have you ever been on the receiving end of prejudice or favoritism? What was the experience like?

4. Is it wrong—always, never, or sometimes—to call in favors and pull strings? How about "networking" in your career or ministry? How likely are you to pour yourself out for or befriend a person who can't help you out?

5. Suppose a Christian friend comes to you and confesses, "I'm feeling convicted. I find myself having contempt for uneducated people. I prefer to be around smart, well-spoken, highly educated people. How can I overcome this?" How would you answer?

6. Look at your answers in the *The "Different" Test*. Which relationships/interactions did you answer as the easiest for you and which the hardest? Do you see a pattern in your answers? What steps can you take or habits can you get into in order to overcome biases toward some people?

Mercy Triumphs

James suggests that a spirit of mercy is the antidote to the sin of prejudice and favoritism. Spend a few minutes prayerfully reading and reflecting on James 2:13: "Judgment without mercy will be

shown to anyone who has not been merciful. Mercy triumphs over judgment." Thinking about God's great mercy for you, journal your thoughts in the space below.

Notes

Notes

3
THE TEST OF
GOOD WORKS

*Faith Is What
We Do*

JAMES 2:14–26

Since the beginning, Christians have argued about confusing spiritual mysteries. Questions like:

- How can God be three (Trinity) and one at the same time?

- How can Jesus be fully human and fully divine?

- Are Christians supposed to be separate from the world or engaged in the world?

James was not afraid to tackle theological conundrums. In fact, it was likely because he waded into the sticky connection between faith and works that some early church leaders questioned the legitimacy of his letter. Some claimed his words contradicted the clear teaching of the apostle Paul, "For it is by grace you have been saved, through faith—and this is not from yourselves, it is the gift of God—not by works so that no one can boast" (Ephesians 2:8–9).

Was James really advocating a different gospel than Paul? And closer to home, how can we live out our faith in ways that honor God and bless others? Let's dive in!

Read It

Key Bible Passage

For this session, read James 2:14–26.

Optional Reading

Read the two Old Testament stories that James mentions:

- Abraham and Isaac in Genesis 22:1–18
- Rahab and the Israelite spies in Joshua 2:1–21

"Faith by itself, if it is not accompanied by action, is dead."

JAMES 2:17

Know It

1. What example does James give of a faith that has no deeds?

2. Check any of the statements below that you would say express James' teaching on the connection between faith and human works (deeds).

   ❏ Faith, unaccompanied by deeds (of love, compassion, etc.) is dead.

   ❏ People are saved by doing good works.

   ❏ Saying "I believe in God/Jesus" proves that we have saving faith.

   ❏ Genuine faith sparks some kind of action on our part.

   ❏ Faith without deeds is useless.

   ❏ We should act as "faith police"—evaluating who is a real Christian.

   ❏ What we believe is revealed by how we live.

3. According to James, how do the story of Abraham and the story of Rahab shed light on the connection between faith and works?

Explore It

Disembodied Faith?

Gnosticism (from the Greek word *gnosis*, which means "knowledge") was an influential belief system from the late first century through the third century. This philosophy emphasized two primary ideas:

1. **Dualism.** This is the belief that all reality is divided into the spiritual and the material. Gnostics regarded the spiritual realm as good and superior to everything material. They viewed material things as earthly and essentially evil. This led to the idea that whatever people choose to do with their bodies (even sinful actions) is irrelevant since only spiritual realities matter.

2. **A desire to "know" ultimate spiritual truth.** Gnostics believed the deep, secret, mysteries of life were known only by a select few. Thus, the goal in Gnosticism had more to do with *knowing* and understanding hidden truth, than with *doing* anything in particular.

Gnosticism wasn't fully developed when James wrote his letter. However, his insistence that faith must express itself through works confronts a gnostic idea that persists even today. That idea is this: a mere mental faith, void of any action or physical expression, is all one needs to please God. James argued that genuine Christian faith results in a new heart that inevitably leads to a new way of living.

Faith and Works

The Bible is clear that we are saved by God's grace alone, through faith alone in Christ alone (Ephesians 2:8–9). Where the tension is felt, and where Christians disagree, is over what happens next. What are the results of salvation? How should (or how does) the gospel alter a heart and a life? What is the connection between faith and works?

Read through the following chart that shows legitimate concerns of believers who, on the one hand, emphasize faith, and those on the other hand, who insist that our lives must show evidence of faith in the form of works.

FAITH	WORKS
Jesus is Savior.	Jesus is Lord.
Emphasizing good works raises the danger of legalism.	Not emphasizing good works raises the danger of license.
Don't make works a requirement.	Don't make works irrelevant.
We are never told to work for our salvation.	We are called to "work out" our salvation (Philippians 2:12–13).
Don't add works to faith.	Don't subtract works from faith.
Believers aren't perfect. Christians sin (1 John 1:8).	New creatures in Christ aren't unchanged (2 Corinthians 5:17). Christians grow and bear fruit.
God is loving and he forgives us.	God is holy and he calls us to righteousness.
Jesus graciously told the woman caught in adultery, "Neither do I condemn you" (John 8:11).	Jesus also told her, "Go now and leave your life of sin" (John 8:11).

FAITH	WORKS
Trust God.	Obey God.
We are saved by faith alone.	Yes, but the faith that saves is never alone.
Be careful—some may hear you saying that it is Christ's sacrifice plus our good works that give us right standing with God.	Be careful—some may hear you saying that it doesn't matter how we live once we put our trust in Christ.
We can't know a person's heart.	Jesus said that the heart will eventually manifest itself on the surface of the life (Matthew 15:19).
Salvation happens in a moment, but transformation into Christ-likeness takes a lifetime.	At some point shouldn't there be signs of transformation?

Love and Deeds

The apostle John, writing a few decades after James, brings up another important connection with deeds: love. He writes, "This is how we know what love is: Jesus Christ laid down his life for us. And we ought to lay down our lives for our brothers and sisters. If anyone has material possessions and sees a brother or sister in need but has no pity on them, how can the love of God be in that person? Dear children, **let us not love with words or speech but with actions and in truth**" (1 John 3:16–18, emphasis added).

Live It

True Faith

James writes about faith taking action. He is not addressing the issue of "saving faith." He is not suggesting that we are made right with God by anything we do. Instead, he writes about the necessity of Christians living out their faith.

We could say it this way: Genuine faith is not merely a noun, something we *have*. It is something we *live*. Biblical faith is a verb. It takes God at his word. It responds. It takes steps. It obeys his will.

True faith looks different in each person's life. But it is ultimately visible. It shows itself. It results in fruit.

The Fruit of the Spirit is . . .

GENTLENESS PATIENCE KINDNESS FAITHFULNESS LOVE JOY SELF-CONTROL PEACE GOODNESS

— Galatians 5:22–23

Life Application Questions

1. Do you think faith and works are enemies or allies? In other words, are they two opposing ideas or two sides of the same coin? Why?

2. Hebrews 11, sometimes known as God's "Faith Hall of Fame," is worth a read. In praising the faith of these individuals, the writer constantly mentions their actions or deeds. What does this suggest to you?

3. Who is someone you admire for how he or she lives out faith in real, tangible ways? How is this person's faith evident?

4. How can you (or any believer) avoid a sterile faith devoid of good works? On the other hand, how can you (or any believer) avoid the dangerous thought that your good works are causing God to like you more?

5. What are the dangers in examining the lives of others for evidence of faith and deeming them "saved" or "not saved" (i.e., true believers or not)?

6. What is your big takeaway from this study? How do you plan to put this truth into practice (James 1:22)?

It's the Small Things

We often think that biblical faith is always epic and heroic—selling all your possessions and giving to the poor, moving to a foreign country to be a missionary, and so forth. But what if God-honoring faith more often involves less dramatic acts?

- Walking across the street to meet your new neighbors—when you are very introverted and shy.

- Calling that coworker who is rightly miffed at you, in order to apologize and mend fences.

- Giving financially to a worthy cause—especially when you could really use the money.

- Initiating a hard conversation with a friend who is heading down a questionable path.

- Signing up for a church class or ministry that will stretch you in hard but good ways.

What might an active, risk-taking faith look like for you this coming week? List three specific and practical actions you can take.

1.

2.

3.

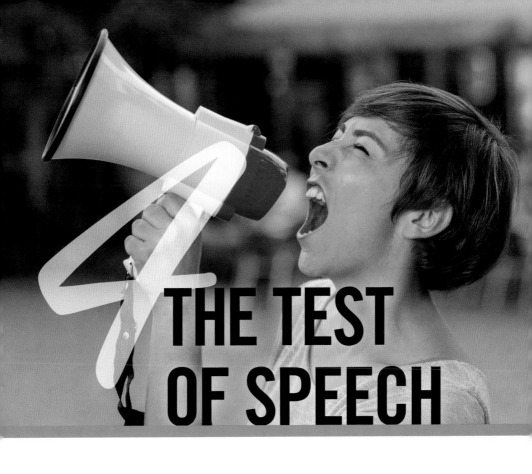

THE TEST
OF SPEECH

*How Words Reveal
the Heart*

JAMES 3:1–12

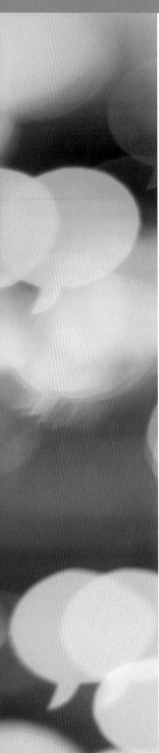

Kathleen Parker of *The Washington Post* tells about an incident that forever marked her life. Her high school English teacher had called on her to identify the parts of a sentence he had written on the blackboard. She was clueless. She hemmed and hawed, and finally blurted out something so clearly wrong that the entire class simultaneously erupted in laughter.

Parker remembers her teacher whirling around to face the class. His face was bright crimson, his voice shaking with anger. "Don't. You. Ever. Laugh. At her. Again," he barked. And then came the sentence that altered her life: "She can out-write every one of you any day of the week."

Parker admitted that she basked in her teacher's words and "in the thought that what he said might be true. I started that day to try to write as well as he said I could. I am still trying."

Who knew that a teacher's kind, encouraging words on one very ordinary day could have such power? In 2010, Kathleen Parker won the coveted Pulitzer Prize for commentary!

With our mouths, we make a powerful difference—either for good or for bad. We can be people who use words to honor God and encourage others, or we can be those who dishonor God and damage others with our words. In this session, we'll look at the test of speech.

Read It

Key Bible Passage

For this session, read James 3:1–12.

Optional Reading

Read these Old Testament proverbs about the power of our words.

Proverbs 12:18–19; 15:4; 17:27–28; 18:21; 26:20

"The tongue is a small part of the body, but it makes great boasts. Consider what a great forest is set on fire by a small spark."

JAMES 3:5

1. What instruction does James give to would-be or wanna-be teachers?

2. What word pictures/imagery does James use to describe the nature of our tongues, especially the way they can set the direction of our lives?

3. What irony about speech does James highlight in 3:9–10?

Bits and Rudders

A *bit* is a small iron bar that is placed in a horse's mouth, between its upper and lower jaws. Connected to a bridle, this literal "bit of metal" gives a hundred-pound jockey the ability to control a massive, thousand-pound thoroughbred horse and turn it whatever direction he or she desires.

Similarly, sailors rely on a *rudder*. A rudder is a flat piece of metal or wood that extends vertically below the surface of the water at the stern (or rear) of a boat. By it a helmsman is able steer the vessel in a chosen direction. Let's say the helmsman causes the rudder to angle to the starboard (the right) side. This causes the water pressure against the rudder to increase on its port (the left) side, and decrease on the right side. Since a boat always moves in

the direction where its rudder faces the least water pressure, the boat will turn to the right.

James uses these images to point out that though our tongues are small, they have a huge influence on the course of our lives.

James and Proverbs

The Bible is full of warnings about the tongue. A large number of these "watch your mouth" passages are found in the Old Testament book of Proverbs. This is fitting since many scholars and Bible readers have likened James' pithy, blunt style to the memorable, concise sayings of King Solomon in Proverbs.

If we had to summarize the message of the Bible regarding our tongues, it would be this: with our mouths, we either make a positive difference or we make a mess.

Some Good Words about Words!

"Kind words do not cost much.
Yet they accomplish so much."
— BLAISE PASCAL

"Saying harsh words is easy.
Unsaying them is impossible."
— UNKNOWN

"Never miss a good chance to shut up."
— WILL ROGERS

MAKING A POSITIVE DIFFERENCE	MAKING A MESS
• Wise speech and faithful instruction Proverbs 10:13; 31:26	• Violent talk Proverbs 10:6
• Nourishing lips Proverbs 10:21	• Lying and slandering Proverbs 10:18; 12:19; 20:14
• Honest and truthful talk Proverbs 12:17, 19; 16:13; 24:26	• Gossip and talking too much Proverbs 11:13; 16:28; 18:8; 20:19; 26:22
• Healing speech Proverbs 12:18; 16:24	• Deceitful and foolish advice Proverbs 12:5; 14:7
• Kind words Proverbs 12:25	• Piercing, hurtful words Proverbs 12:18
• Knowledgeable speech Proverbs 15:7; 19:27; 20:15; 23:12	• Rash speech Proverbs 13:3
• Gentle answers Proverbs 15:1; 25:15	• Boasting and proud talk Proverbs 14:3; 27:2
• A soothing tongue Proverbs 15:4	• Harsh words Proverbs 15:1
• Aptly-spoken or well-timed words Proverbs 15:23; 25:11	• Quarreling Proverbs 17:14, 19; 20:3
• Gracious words Proverbs 15:26; 16:21, 24	• Perverse talk Proverbs 19:1
• Sharing good news Proverbs 15:30	• Mocking and insulting Proverbs 22:10
• Restrained speech Proverbs 17:27	• Exaggeration Proverbs 22:13; 26:13
	• Disingenuous speech and flattery Proverbs 26:24; 29:5

"The Mouth Bone's Connected to the . . . "

Most people have heard the famous (and silly) kids' song titled "Dem Bones." It teaches basic anatomy and includes lyrics like these: "The hip bone's connected to the backbone. The backbone's connected to the neck bone. The neck bone's connected to the head bone" . . . and on and on.

The Bible however highlights a different connection—a spiritual one between the mouth and heart. Consider the words of Jesus:

> ## "What you say flows from what is in your heart."
>
> Luke 6:45 NLT

Controlling an Uncontrollable Tongue

What do each of the following Bible verses suggest about how we can "get a grip" on our tongues? (The first one is supplied as an example.)

BIBLE VERSES	POINT OR PRINCIPLE
"Above all else, guard your heart, for everything you do flows from it" (Proverbs 4:23).	*If my heart isn't right, my speech won't be either.*
"May these words of my mouth and this meditation of my heart be pleasing in your sight, LORD, my Rock and my Redeemer" (Psalm 19:14).	
"Set a guard over my mouth, LORD; keep watch over the door of my lips" (Psalm 141:3).	
"Those who consider themselves religious and yet do not keep a tight rein on their tongues deceive themselves, and their religion is worthless" (James 1:26).	

BIBLE VERSES	POINT OR PRINCIPLE
"Do not offer any part of yourself to sin as an instrument of wickedness, but rather offer yourselves to God as those who have been brought from death to life; and offer every part of yourself to him as an instrument of righteousness" (Romans 6:13).	
"Those who guard their mouths and their tongues keep themselves from calamity" (Proverbs 21:23).	
"My dear brothers and sisters, take note of this: Everyone should be quick to listen, slow to speak and slow to become angry" (James 1:19).	

Live It

Speech Habits

Think of a setting in which you spend a lot of time with others. Circle only one below.

Workplace   A ministry/volunteer team

School   Home with family/roommates

With my group of friends   Other: _____

What if you had a video recording of your particular group's interactions from the last seven days? Check any of the following verbal actions it might show people engaging in.

- ❏ Using profanity
- ❏ Complimenting
- ❏ Complaining
- ❏ Bragging
- ❏ Criticizing
- ❏ Gossiping
- ❏ Comforting
- ❏ Lying
- ❏ Encouraging
- ❏ Interrupting
- ❏ Defusing a tense situation

- ❏ Praising God
- ❏ Expressing thanks
- ❏ Threatening
- ❏ Yelling
- ❏ Instructing
- ❏ Reminding
- ❏ Nagging
- ❏ Exaggerating
- ❏ Sharing uplifting news
- ❏ Arguing
- ❏ Joking/laughing

If you had to assign a grade (A, B, C, D, or F) to your group's overall speech habits, what grade would you give?

GROUP REPORT CARD

Grade:

A   B   C   D   F

Now consider this: What would the camera catch you saying? How would you grade yourself?

YOUR REPORT CARD

Grade:

A   B   C   D   F

Life Application Questions

1. Can you think of a specific instance when someone impacted you for good by speaking words of life into your soul? What made his or her words so memorable?

2. Kids like to parrot the little saying, "Sticks and stones can break my bones, but words can never hurt me." Do you agree with this sentiment? Why or why not?

3. Who is a person you admire for the way they interact verbally with others? Why?

4. How might the Bible's warnings about speech also apply to the things we "say" on social media? Is there something that needs to change about your words online?

5. Do you agree that the tongue and the heart are closely linked? How do you see this in your own life?

6. Suppose a friend confided in you, "I need some help. I've developed a foul mouth and I can't seem to get it under control. How can I unlearn my bad habits?" How would you respond?

Personal Reflection

In what specific ways have you used your words for good? In what specific ways has your mouth been an "instrument of unrighteousness" (Romans 6:13)? You may also want to use the list of verses from Proverbs earlier in this session as a guide.

After a time of personal reflection . . .

- Confess your verbal sins and shortcomings to God (1 John 1:9).

- Thank him for the forgiveness provided in Christ.

- Pray for the grace to truly turn away today from all verbal sin.

- Invite the Spirit of Almighty God to fill you, empower you, and guard your speech, recognizing that in your own power, "no one can tame the tongue" (James 3:8).

If you realize you have spoken harshly to others, engaged in petty quarrels or "unwholesome talk" (Ephesians 4:29), said things that weren't true, and so on, use your tongue to rectify those sins of the tongue.

- Go and humbly admit your sin to those you have wronged. Express your sorrow. Say, "I'm sorry. Will you forgive me?"

Notes

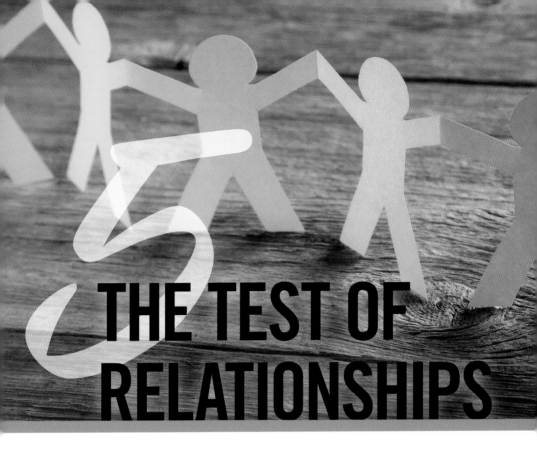

THE TEST OF RELATIONSHIPS

The Challenge of Community

JAMES 3:13–5:6

A sharp, young college graduate was hired by a large, public middle school to teach seventh grade math. After one year, she announced she was "retiring" from teaching in order to pursue a degree in accounting. She explained, "I absolutely loved teaching. Everything about it—well, except for the part of having to deal with all those students!"

We shake our heads in laughter. Then we nod knowingly. People are difficult. They make us crazy! But as James (and the rest of the Bible) teaches, God can also use those same people to make us more like Jesus.

Read It

Key Bible Passage

For this session, read James 3:13–5:6.

Optional Reading

Read about the value of wisdom in Proverbs 2.

"The wisdom that comes from heaven is first of all pure; then peace-loving, considerate, submissive, full of mercy and good fruit, impartial and sincere."

JAMES 3:17

Know It

1. What is the difference between earthly wisdom and God's wisdom in James 3:13–18?

2. According to James 4:1–18, what are some of the underlying attitudes that create many of the problems in our relationships and lives?

3. What special warning does James give the wealthy hoarders and cheaters in 5:1–6?

Heaven's Wisdom

In the rest of the Bible (and here in James too), *wisdom* is more than intelligence. We all know smart people—those with high IQs, good GPAs, lots of knowledge—who nevertheless act foolishly in many real-life situations. More than knowing facts, wisdom is understanding people and situations and seeing the right and best ways to succeed.

This is the "wisdom that comes from heaven" (James 3:17). Since God is all-wise, he is the ultimate source for this vital insight. The more we look up to him, especially in the midst of trying human interactions, the more we learn how to respond with wisdom.

Wisdom

LANGUAGE	WORD	DEFINITION
Hebrew	*hokmah*	skill in living, shrewdness, prudence
Greek	*sophia*	insight, skill (human or divine), intelligence, clarity

Real Peace

James writes that godly wisdom brings peace. When we think of *peace*, we often think of the lack of overt conflict: "Are things peaceful at my house? Well, there are no fists or frying pans flying around . . . so, yeah, I guess so. For today at least."

Biblical peace is so much more than this. The Hebrew word for *peace*—a word that James would have known intimately and used often—is the word *shalom*. It's a beautiful word, rich in meaning. *Shalom* isn't merely the absence of friction and fighting, it's the presence of all things good! *Shalom* means fullness and wholeness, vitality and fruitfulness. *Shalom* is synonymous with joy, health, prosperity, and safety. God's peace—the *shalom* he wants for his people—is life the way it was meant to be.

"Peacemakers will plant seeds of peace and reap a harvest of righteousness."

JAMES 3:18 NLT

"But I'm Not Wealthy!"

James 5:1–6 is addressed to "you rich people." Maybe you read that and are thinking, "Obviously, that doesn't apply to me. I'm anything but rich." Not so fast. We have to remember that wealth is relative. In fact, according to *Global Rich List*, if you make just $18,000 a year, you're wealthier than 95% of the people in the world! Check out www.globalrichlist.com for yourself to see where your income lands.

James is not condemning wealth, per se. Rather, just as in other biblical texts about riches, James calls to account those who have financial means and hoard their wealth, cheat their workers, and turn a deaf ear to those in need. Material wealth, though a blessing, can become a great curse. When we set our hearts on earthly things and look to our riches to give us life, nobody wins.

Live It

Wise or Foolish?

James distinguishes between the wisdom that comes from above and earthly wisdom. He says the former, God's wisdom, is marked by understanding, humility, and purity. It is peace-loving, considerate, submissive, full of mercy, impartial and sincere. The "wisdom" of the world, on the other hand, is marked by "bitter envy and selfish ambition" (3:14). It denies the truth—God's truth—and is unspiritual, even of the devil.

How might heavenly wisdom and earthly wisdom respond differently to each of the following situations?

SITUATION	Your new neighbor has a rock band that practices loudly till late every night. When you go to talk with him about the noise, he just shrugs and says, "It's a free country."
WORLDLY RESPONSE	
GODLY RESPONSE	

SITUATION	A wild driver passes you on the shoulder on the expressway, almost causing you to wreck, and making you miss your exit.
WORLDLY RESPONSE	
GODLY RESPONSE	

SITUATION	Your church has a new pastor—and you don't like his sermons.
WORLDLY RESPONSE	
GODLY RESPONSE	

SITUATION	Your spouse is spending excessive amounts of time at work and on his or her hobbies. You two are growing distant.
WORLDLY RESPONSE	
GODLY RESPONSE	

Life Application Questions

1. According to James, coveting is one source of friction between people (4:2). When has this been true in your experience?

2. How would you describe what it means to be someone who "cultivates peace" (3:18)? Share about a time when you've seen or been part of cultivating peace between people.

3. How much peace (*shalom*) do you have currently in your life and relationships?

4. Do an autopsy of the last argument you had. What were the surface issues? What were the deeper issues?

5. Think back over all you've learned from the book of James so far. In light of that, what does it mean to live wisely— particularly in relationships?

6. What does it look like—practically and realistically—to "submit to God" (4:7) and "come near to God" (4:8)? How can other believers help you take these steps? And how can you help them?

Pride and Humility

James speaks often about the importance of humility. He reminds us that "God opposes the proud" (4:6).

If the history of humanity tells us anything, it's this: Pride is destructive to relationships. Pride is the exaltation of self. Pride is self-serving. Self-seeking. Self-centered. Self-obsessed. Self-absorbed. Pride says, "me . . . Me! . . . ME!" Pride demands, "I want attention and praise. I want to be right. I want my way. I want others to *get out of my way*. I want whatever I want, whenever I want it."

Spend a few minutes quietly asking God to show you any instances of pride in your relationships. If/when he does, confess those things. Claim the forgiveness readily available in Jesus. Ask the Spirit of God to give you a spirit of humility.

Notes

Notes

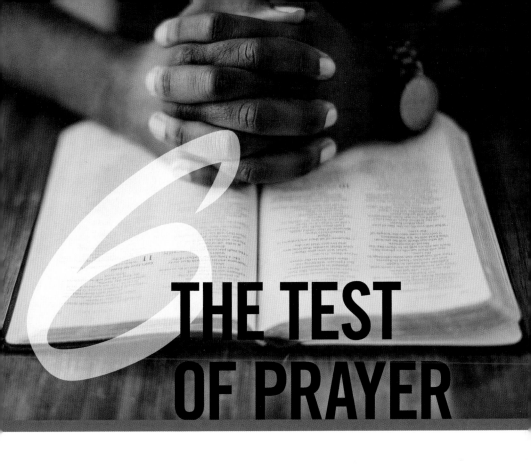

THE TEST
OF PRAYER

*What to Do
in Hard Times*

JAMES 5:7–20

James finishes his short letter in pretty much the same way he began: by talking about difficulty, struggles, and testing. But his point isn't just that we should expect such troubles. Rather his exhortation is for us to "be patient and stand firm" (5:8). When? "In the face of suffering" (5:10).

And while we patiently wait? We are to *pray.* We are to turn our faces, our hearts, and our lives toward the One who is "full of compassion and mercy" (5:11).

Read It

Key Bible Passage

For this session, read James' closing remarks in James 5:7–20.

Optional Reading

Read the story of Elijah that James mentions.

1 Kings 17:1–7; 18:41–45

"The prayer of a righteous person is powerful and effective."

JAMES 5:16

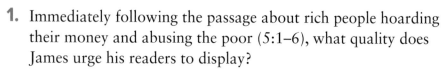

Know It

1. Immediately following the passage about rich people hoarding their money and abusing the poor (5:1–6), what quality does James urge his readers to display?

2. According to verse 9, what is one of the telltale indicators of impatience?

3. What specific instructions does James give about prayer and praise?

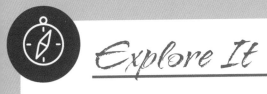

Explore It

Around-the-Clock Prayers

James says that we should look to God not just when we are "in trouble" (5:13) or when we're "sick" (5:14), or when we need to "confess" some wrong act (5:16), but also when we're "happy" (5:13). That seems to cover most situations in life!

This pray-all-the-time mindset mirrors the Psalms, Israel's great prayer/hymn book. It has been pointed out that most of the 150 psalms seem to say either:

- "Thanks!"—an appreciation for some divine blessing,

- "Wow!"—a praise to God for his glory and beauty, or

- "Help!"—laments or confessions or requests for divine help.

Again, these three categories cover most circumstances in life.

Consider what the apostle Paul says in Ephesians 6:18: "Pray in the Spirit *on all occasions* with all kinds of prayers and requests. With this in mind, be alert and *always keep on praying* for all the Lord's people." In 1 Thessalonians 5:17, Paul urges, "pray *continually*." And in Philippians 4:6–7 we read, "Do not be anxious about anything, but in *every situation*, by prayer and petition, with thanksgiving, present your requests to God. And the peace of God, which transcends all understanding, will guard your hearts and your minds in Christ Jesus" (Philippians 4:6). (Emphasis added.)

In other words, prayer isn't to be some last resort when things are dire. It's to be around-the-clock and for all of life.

Biblical Patience

A major theme from the entire letter of James is endurance—and specifically in chapter five, endurance *in prayer*. Prayer typically involves waiting, doesn't it? We pour out our hearts to God, then wait for him to work his will, in his way, and according to his timetable. The more we trust the heart of God the easier it is to wait patiently for him to act.

James urges his readers to be patient, like a farmer waiting for rain to come. The Greek verb for patience *makrothumeo*, and it has to do with exhibiting internal and external control while facing hard circumstances. In previous generations, Christians referred to this virtue as *longsuffering*. This is a calmness, born of faith, that enables one to wait, and keeps one from angry irritation. Patient people don't "get riled up." They don't blow their stacks, fly off the handle, or flip their lids. Rather, they bear tough trials and endure delays graciously, without grumbling or acting rashly.

"See how the farmer waits for the land to yield its valuable crop. . . . You too, be patient and stand firm."

JAMES 5:7–8

Live It

The "Old Soul" on Trials and Suffering

George MacDonald was a nineteenth century Scottish minister and author whose prolific writings had a major influence on C. S. Lewis. MacDonald's devotional book *The Diary of an Old Soul* is a modern classic, featuring 365 prayer-poems, one for each day of the year.

One prayer (for October 2) speaks of our need to submit patiently to God's refining, shaping work in our lives even when we don't know what he is doing—and how doing so leads to new grace and strength.

> But thou art making me,
>   I thank thee, sire.
>
> What thou hast done and doest thou
>   know'st well,
>
> And I will help thee:—gently in thy fire
>
> I will lie burning; on thy potter's-wheel
>
> I will whirl patient, though my brain
>   should reel;
>
> Thy grace shall be enough
>   the grief to quell,
>
> And growing strength perfect through
>   weakness dire.

Consider the imagery in MacDonald's poem: being refined in a fire and shaped like clay on a potter's wheel. They're images from the Bible.

- "These trials will show that your faith is genuine. It is being tested as fire tests and purifies gold" (1 Peter 1:7 NLT).

- "You, LORD, are our Father. We are the clay, you are the potter; we are all the work of your hand" (Isaiah 64:8).

Our loving Creator is making us into who he wants us to be!

Life Application Questions

1. What are some long-term prayer requests you've been offering up to God? Are you feeling patient or impatient?

2. It's been said that God answers all prayers with either *yes, no,* or *not yet.* Do you think this is accurate? Why or why not?

3. In verse 16, James urges believers to "confess your sins to each other." Why is even the thought of confession so hard and scary for most folks? What are the risks and blessings if we do confess to one another? What are the dangers if we don't participate in this spiritual practice?

4. What does confessing to each other look like in practical terms? For example, in one-on-one meetings, in small groups, or during large congregational meetings?

5. Have you ever been helped by fellow believers when you "wandered from the truth"—or been the person who helped bring a wanderer back? Did prayer play a role in that process? What did you learn from that experience?

6. Reflect back on all six sessions of this study on the book of James. What insights or takeaways resonated with you the most? Why?

A Prayer from Your Heart

Look again at George MacDonald's poem in this session. Could you genuinely pray this prayer from your heart, thanking God for the way he is making you into the image of his Son? Surrendering to whatever he might be doing in and through you via your trials? Trusting that his strength and grace will see you through?

In the space below, write a prayer or poem to the Lord, asking him to refine your faith like gold and shape your life like clay.

Notes

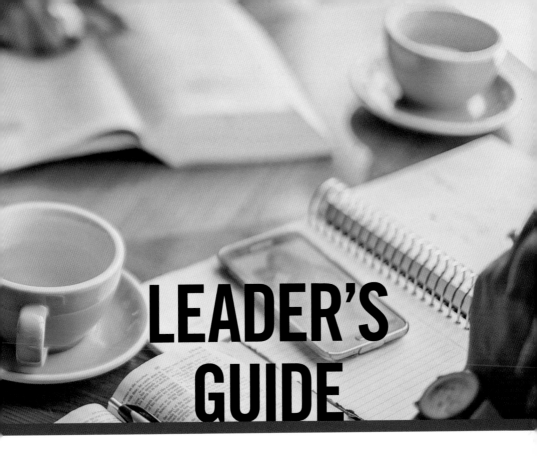

LEADER'S GUIDE

"Encourage one another and build each other up."

1 THESSALONIANS 5:11

Leader's Guide

Congratulations! You've either decided to lead a Bible study, or you're thinking hard about it. Guess what? God does big things through small groups. When his people gather together, open his Word, and invite his Spirit to work, their lives are changed!

Do you feel intimidated yet?

Be comforted by this: even the great apostle Paul felt "in over his head" at times. When he went to Corinth to help people grasp God's truth, he admitted he was overwhelmed: "I came to you in weakness with great fear and trembling" (1 Corinthians 2:3). Later he wondered, "Who is adequate for such a task as this?" (2 Corinthians 2:16 NLT).

Feelings of inadequacy are normal; every leader has them. What's more, they're actually healthy. They keep us dependent on the Lord. It is in our times of greatest weakness that God works most powerfully. The Lord assured Paul, "My grace is sufficient for you, for my power is made perfect in weakness" (2 Corinthians 12:9).

The Goal

What is the goal of a Bible study group? Listen as the apostle Paul speaks to Christians:

- "Oh, my dear children! I feel as if I'm going through labor pains for you again, and they will continue until *Christ is fully developed in your lives*" (Galatians 4:19 NLT, emphasis added).

- "For God knew his people in advance, and he chose them *to become like his Son*" (Romans 8:29 NLT, emphasis added).

Do you see it? God's ultimate goal for us is that we would become like Jesus Christ. This means a Bible study is not about filling our heads with more information. Rather, it is about undergoing transformation. We study and apply God's truth so that it will reshape our hearts and minds, and so that, over time we will become more and more like Jesus.

Paul said, "The purpose of my instruction is that all believers would be filled with love that comes from a pure heart, a clear conscience, and genuine faith" (1 Timothy 1:5 NLT).

This isn't about trying to "master the Bible." No, we're praying that God's Word will master us, and through humble submission to its authority, we'll be changed from the inside out.

Your Role

Many group leaders experience frustration because they confuse their role with God's role. Here's the truth: God alone knows our deep hang-ups and hurts. Only he can save a soul, heal a heart, fix a life. It is God who rescues people from depression, addictions, bitterness, guilt, and shame. We Bible study leaders need to realize that *we can't do any of those things.*

So what can we do? More than we think!

- We can pray.

- We can trust God to work powerfully.

- We can obey the Spirit's promptings.

- We can prepare for group gatherings.

- We can keep showing up faithfully.

With group members:

- We can invite, remind, encourage, and love.

- We can ask good questions and then listen attentively.

- We can gently speak tough truths.

- We can celebrate with those who are happy and weep with those who are sad.

- We can call and text and let them know we've got their back.

But we can never do the things that only the Almighty can do.

- We can't play the Holy Spirit in another person's life.

- We can't be in charge of outcomes.

- We can't force God to work according to our timetables.

And one more important reminder: besides God's role and our role, group members also have a key role to play in this process. If they don't show up, prepare, or open their hearts to God's transforming truth, no life change will take place. We're not called to manipulate or shame, pressure or arm twist. We're not to blame if members don't make progress—and we don't get the credit when they do. We're mere instruments in the hands of God.

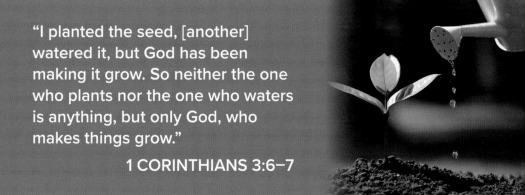

"I planted the seed, [another] watered it, but God has been making it grow. So neither the one who plants nor the one who waters is anything, but only God, who makes things grow."

1 CORINTHIANS 3:6–7

Leader Myths and Truths

Many people assume that a Bible study leader should:

- Be a Bible scholar.

- Be a dynamic communicator.

- Have a big, fancy house to meet in.

- Have it all together—no doubts, bad habits, or struggles.

These are myths—even outright lies of the enemy!

Here's the truth:

- God is looking for humble Bible students, not scholars.

- You're not signing up to give lectures, you're agreeing to facilitate discussions.

- You don't need a palace, just a place where you can have uninterrupted discussions. (Perhaps one of your group members will agree to host your study.)

- Nobody has it all together. We are all in process. We are all seeking to work out "our salvation with fear and trembling" (Philippians 2:12).

As long as your desire is that Jesus be Lord of your life, God will use you!

Some Bad Reasons to Lead a Group

- You want to wow others with your biblical knowledge.

  "Love . . . does not boast, it is not proud"
  (1 Corinthians 13:4).

- You're seeking a hidden personal gain or profit.

  "We do not peddle the word of God for profit"
  (2 Corinthians 2:17).

- You want to tell people how wrong they are.

  "Do not condemn" (Romans 2:1).

- You want to fix or rescue people.

  "It is God who works in you to will and to act"
  (Philippians 2:13).

- You're being pressured to do it.

  "Am I now trying to win the approval of
  human beings, or of God?" (Galatians 1:10).

A Few Do's

✔ Pray for your group.

Are you praying for your group members regularly? It is the most important thing a leader can do for his or her group.

✔ Ask for help.

If you're new at leading, spend time with an experienced group leader and pick his or her brain.

✔ Encourage members to prepare.

Challenge participants to read the Bible passages and the material in their study guides, and to answer and reflect on the study questions during the week prior to meeting.

✔ Discuss the group guidelines.

Go over important guidelines with your group at the first session, and again as needed if new members join the group in later sessions. See the *Group Guidelines* at the end of this leader's guide.

✔ Share the load.

Don't be a one-person show. Ask for volunteers. Let group members host the meeting, arrange for snacks, plan socials, lead group prayer times, and so forth. The old saying is true: Participants become boosters; spectators become critics.

✔ Be flexible.

If a group member shows up in crisis, it is okay to stop and take time to surround the hurting brother or sister with love. Provide a safe place for sharing. Listen and pray for his or her needs.

✔ Be kind.

Remember, there's a story—often a heart-breaking one—behind every face. This doesn't *excuse* bad or disruptive behavior on the part of group members, but it might *explain* it.

A Few Don'ts

✘ Don't "wing it."

Although these sessions are designed to require minimum preparation, read each one ahead of time. Highlight the questions you feel are especially important for your group to spend time on.

✘ Don't feel ashamed to say, "I don't know."

Disciple means "learner," not "know-it-all."

✘ Don't feel the need to "dump the truck."

You don't have to say everything you know. There is always next week. A little silence during group discussion time, that's fine. Let members wrestle with questions.

✘ Don't put members on the spot.

Invite others to share and pray, but don't pressure them. Give everyone an opportunity to participate. People will open up on their own time as they learn to trust the group.

✘ Don't go down "rabbit trails."

Be careful not to let one person dominate the time or for the discussion to go down the gossip road. At the same time, don't short-circuit those occasions when the Holy Spirit is working in your group members' lives and therefore they *need* to share a lot.

✘ Don't feel pressure to cover every question.

Better to have a robust discussion of four questions than a superficial conversation of ten.

✘ Don't go long.

Encourage good discussion, but don't be afraid to "rope 'em back in" when needed. Start and end on time. If you do this from the beginning, you'll avoid the tendency of group members to arrive later and later as the season goes on.

How to Use This Study Guide

Many group members have busy lives—dealing with long work hours, childcare, and a host of other obligations. These sessions are designed to be as simple and straightforward as possible to fit into a busy schedule. Nevertheless, encourage group members to set aside some time during the week (even if it's only a little) to pray, read the key Bible passage, and respond to questions in this study guide. This will make the group discussion and experience much more rewarding for everyone.

Each session contains four parts.

Read It

The *Key Bible Passage* is the portion of Scripture everyone should read during the week before the group meeting. The group can read it together at the beginning of the session as well.

The *Optional Reading* is for those who want to dig deeper and read lengthier Bible passages on their own during the week.

Know It

This section encourages participants to reflect on the Bible passage they've just read. Here, the goal is to interact with the biblical text and grasp what it says. (We'll get into practical application later.)

Explore It

Here group members can find background information with charts and visuals to help them understand the Bible passage and the topic more deeply. They'll move beyond the text itself and see how it connects to other parts of Scripture and the historical and cultural context.

Live It

Finally, participants will examine how God's Word connects to their lives. There are application questions for group discussion or personal reflection, practical ideas to apply what they've learned from God's Word, and a closing thought and/or prayer. (Remember, you don't have to cover all the questions or everything in this section during group time. Focus on what's most important for your group.)

Celebrate!

Here's an idea: Have a plan for celebrating your time together after the last session of this Bible study. Do something special after your gathering time, or plan a separate celebration for another time and place. Maybe someone in your group has the gift of hospitality—let them use their gifting and organize the celebration.

	30-MINUTE SESSION	60-MINUTE SESSION
READ IT	Open in prayer and read the *Key Bible Passage.* 5 minutes	Open in prayer and read the *Key Bible Passage.* 5 minutes
KNOW IT	Ask: "What stood out to you from this Bible passage?" 5 minutes	Ask: "What stood out to you from this Bible passage?" 5 minutes
EXPLORE IT	Encourage group members to read this section on their own, but don't spend group time on it. Move on to the life application questions.	Ask: "What did you find new or helpful in the *Explore It* section? What do you still have questions about?" 10 minutes
LIVE IT	Members voluntarily share their answers to 3 or 4 of the life application questions. 15 minutes	Members voluntarily share their answers to the life application questions. 25 minutes
PRAYER & CLOSING	Conclude with a brief prayer. 5 minutes	Share prayer requests and praise reports. Encourage the group to pray for each other in the coming week. Conclude with a brief prayer. 15 minutes

90-MINUTE SESSION

Open in prayer and read the *Key Bible Passage.*

5 minutes

- Ask: "What stood out to you from this Bible passage?"
- Then go over the *Know It* questions as a group.

10 minutes

- Ask: "What did you find new or helpful in the *Explore It* section? What do you still have questions about?"
- Here, the leader can add information found while preparing for the session.
- If there are questions or a worksheet in this section, go over those as a group.

20 minutes

- Members voluntarily share their answers to the life application questions.
- Wrap up this time with a closing thought or suggestions for how to put into practice in the coming week what was just learned from God's Word.

30 minutes

- Share prayer requests and praise reports.
- Members voluntarily pray during group time about the requests and praises shared.
- Encourage the group to pray for each other in the coming week.

25 minutes

Group Guidelines

This group is about discovering God's truth, supporting each other, and finding growth in our new life in Christ. To reach these goals, a group needs a few simple guidelines that everyone should follow for the group to stay healthy and for trust to develop.

1. **Everyone agrees to make group time a priority.**
   We understand that there are work, health, and family issues that come up. So if there is an emergency or schedule conflict that cannot be avoided, be sure to let someone know that you can't make it that week. This may seem like a small thing, but it makes a big difference to your other group members.

2. **What is said in the group stays in the group.**
   Accept it now: we are going to share some personal things. Therefore, the group must be a safe and confidential place to share.

3. **Don't be judgmental, even if you strongly disagree.**
   Listen first, and contribute your perspective only as needed. Remember, you don't fully know someone else's story. Take this advice from James: "Be quick to listen, slow to speak, and slow to become angry" (James 1:19).

4. **Be patient with one another.**
   We are all in process, and some of us are hurting and struggling more than others. Don't expect bad habits or attitudes to disappear overnight.

5. **Everyone participates.**
   It may take time to learn how to share, but as you develop a trust toward the other group members, take the chance.

If you struggle in any of these areas, ask God's help for growth, and ask the group to help hold you accountable. Remember, you're all growing together.

Notes

Notes

ROSE VISUAL BIBLE STUDIES
6-Session Study Guides for Personal or Group Use

Rose Visual Bible Studies are packed with full-color visuals that show key information at a glance! With their easy-to-use format—*read it, know it, explore it,* and *live it*—these 6-week inductive studies are perfect for gaining a deeper insight into God's Word.

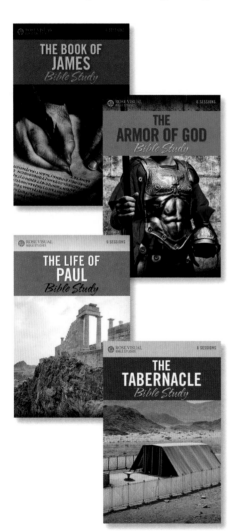

THE BOOK OF JAMES
Find out what James says about cultivating a genuine living faith through six tests of faith: trials, favoritism, good works, speech, relationships, and prayer.
ISBN 9781628627589

THE ARMOR OF GOD
Dig deep into Ephesians 6 and learn the meaning of each piece of the armor, its historical uses, and its application to spiritual battles today.
ISBN 9781628627558

THE LIFE OF PAUL
From his conversion on the road to Damascus to his martyrdom in Rome, see how the apostle Paul persevered through trials and fearlessly proclaimed the gospel of Jesus.
ISBN 9781628627619

THE TABERNACLE
From the golden lampstand to the ark of the covenant, discover how each item of the tabernacle foreshadowed Jesus and what that means for us today.
ISBN 9781628627527